COMPARING ANIMAL TRAITS

EMPEROR PENGUINS

ANTARCTIC DIVING BIRDS

LAURA HAMILTON WAXMAN

Lerner Publications ◆ Minneapolis

For Anita, mother and grandmother extraordinaire

Lerner Publications Company
A division of Lerner Publishing Group, Inc.
241 First Avenue North
Minneapolis, MN 55401 USA

For reading levels and more information, look up this title at www.lernerbooks.com.

Photo Acknowledgments

The images in this book are used with the permission of: © iStockphoto.com/Coldimages, p. 1; © Radius Images/Alamy, p. 4; © Paul Nicklen/National Geographic/Getty Images, pp. 5, 7 (bottom), 8; © Peace Portal Photo/Alamy, p. 6; © Wolfgang Kaehler/Getty Images, pp. 7 (top), 11 (left); © blickwinkel/Alamy, pp. 9 (top left), 15 (right), 27 (bottom); © Volt Collection/Shutterstock.com, p. 9 (bottom); © iStockphoto.com/ AndreAnita, p. 9 (top right); © Alan Murphy, BIA/Minden Pictures, p. 10; © Tom Vezo/Minden Pictures, p. 11 (right); © Laura Westlund/Independent Picture Service, p. 12; © All Canada Photos/Alamy, pp. 13, 19 (bottom), 20, 22; © Tui De Roy/naturepl.com, p. 14; © Photoshot Holdings Ltd/Alamy, p. 15 (left); © Steve Bloom Images/SuperStock, p. 16; © iStockphoto.com/Roberto A. Sanchez, p. 17; © Nature Picture Library/ Alamy, p. 18; © John Digby/Alamy, p. 19 (top);© Jan Vermeer/Minden/Getty Images, p. 21 (bottom left); © Glenn Bartley/All Canada Photos/Getty Images, p. 21 (bottom right); © Don Mammoser/Alamy, p. 23; © Doug Allan/Getty Images, p. 24; © Steve Bloom Images/Alamy, p. 25; © Bill Bachman/Alamy, p. 26; © Auscape/UIG/Getty Images, p. 27 (top); © iStockphoto.com/Angela Arenal, p. 28; © Keren Su/China Span/Alamy, p. 29 (left); © DansPhotoArt/Moment Open/Getty Images, p. 29 (right).

Front cover: © iStockphoto.com/KeithSzafranski.
Back cover: © Jan Martin Will/Shutterstock.com.

Main body text set in Calvert MT Std 12/18. Typeface provided by Monotype Typography.

Library of Congress Cataloging-in-Publication Data

Waxman, Laura Hamilton.
   Emperor penguins : Antarctic diving birds / Laura Hamilton Waxman.
      pages cm. — (Comparing animal traits)
    Includes bibliographical references and index.
    Audience: Ages 7 to 10.
    Audience: Grades K to grade 3.
    ISBN 978-1-4677-9505-0 (lb : alk. paper) — ISBN 978-1-4677-9625-5 (pb : alk. paper) —
ISBN 978-1-4677-9626-2 (eb pdf)
    1. Emperor penguin—Juvenile literature. I. Title.
  QL696.S473W395 2015
  598.47—dc23   2015015766

Manufactured in the United States of America
1 – BP – 12/31/15

TABLE OF CONTENTS

INTRODUCTION

MEET THE EMPEROR PENGUIN

A hungry emperor penguin plunges into the icy ocean. A powerful swimmer, the penguin dives deep in search of fish to eat. Emperor penguins are a kind of bird. Birds are animals. Other kinds of animals you may know are fish, insects, reptiles, amphibians, and mammals.

Emperor penguins live in Antarctica.

All birds share certain traits. Birds are vertebrates—animals with backbones. Birds are covered with feathers. They also have two wings and a beak. Birds are warm-blooded. Their bodies keep a steady temperature regardless of the surrounding temperature. Birds lay hard-shelled eggs. The emperor penguin shares these traits with other birds. It also has traits that make it unique.

CHAPTER 1

WHAT DO EMPEROR PENGUINS LOOK LIKE?

Emperor penguins are big birds. They're the world's largest penguin **species**. Emperor penguins stand about 45 inches (115 centimeters) tall. They can weigh more than 80 pounds (36 kilograms). That's about as much as some eleven-year-old children! Most birds weigh less, which helps them fly. But penguins can't fly.

Layers of feathers keep emperor penguins warm and dry.

Thick layers of feathers cover an emperor penguin's body. The feathers help keep the bird warm. An emperor penguin's feathers are black on the back, head, and wings. Its belly feathers are white. The top of its chest is orange. An oily coating on penguin feathers makes them waterproof. The tips of the feathers overlap like shingles on a roof. This helps keep out water.

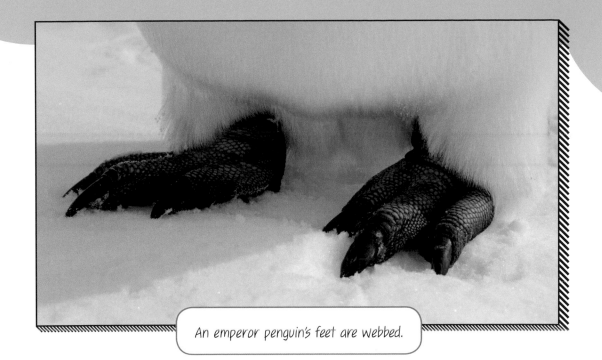

An emperor penguin's feet are webbed.

An emperor penguin's body is well-suited for swimming. Its wings are flat and shaped like flippers. The bird has thick, sturdy legs with webbed feet. Its body is long and oval to help it glide through the water. It has a short neck and a large head.

DID YOU KNOW?

Most birds have **HOLLOW** bones. Hollow bones weigh less and make it easier for birds to fly. But an emperor penguin's bones are solid and heavy. Being heavy helps emperor penguins sink deep underwater.

EMPEROR PENGUINS VS. ROYAL PENGUINS

A royal penguin waddles down a rocky slope to the beach. This type of penguin spends most of its life on Macquarie Island, south of New Zealand. Royal penguins have long, streamlined bodies, just like emperor penguins. This body shape helps them zoom through the water. Royal penguins also have short necks and big heads. Like emperor penguins, royal penguins swim with their flat wings. Both penguins stand upright on two thick legs and webbed feet.

Royal penguins

Emperor penguins (*left*) look very similar to royal penguins (*right*).

Royal penguins and emperor penguins are similar in color. They're both black on the back and white on the belly. This coloring helps to **camouflage** the penguins in the water. Their white bellies blend in with the lighter water above them. Their black backs blend in with the darker water below them.

DID YOU KNOW?
There are **SEVENTEEN** penguin species. They vary in size and weight. They all have dark backs, white bellies, and long bodies.

EMPEROR PENGUINS VS. PAINTED BUNTINGS

A painted bunting flies into a tree and perches on a branch. Painted buntings live in southern parts of North America. They are much smaller than emperor penguins. Painted buntings are only about 5 inches (13 cm) long. Adults weigh as much as 0.7 ounces (20 grams) and as little as 0.5 ounces (14 g). That's less than three nickels!

Unlike emperor penguins, painted buntings can be quite colorful. Female painted buntings are mostly green. Males are bright blue, red, yellow, and green.

Painted buntings don't have webbed feet like emperor penguins do. Painted buntings have four separate toes for perching on branches. Their wings have long, light feathers. The fluffy feathers are suited for flying instead of swimming.

A male painted bunting eats a berry.

COMPARE IT!

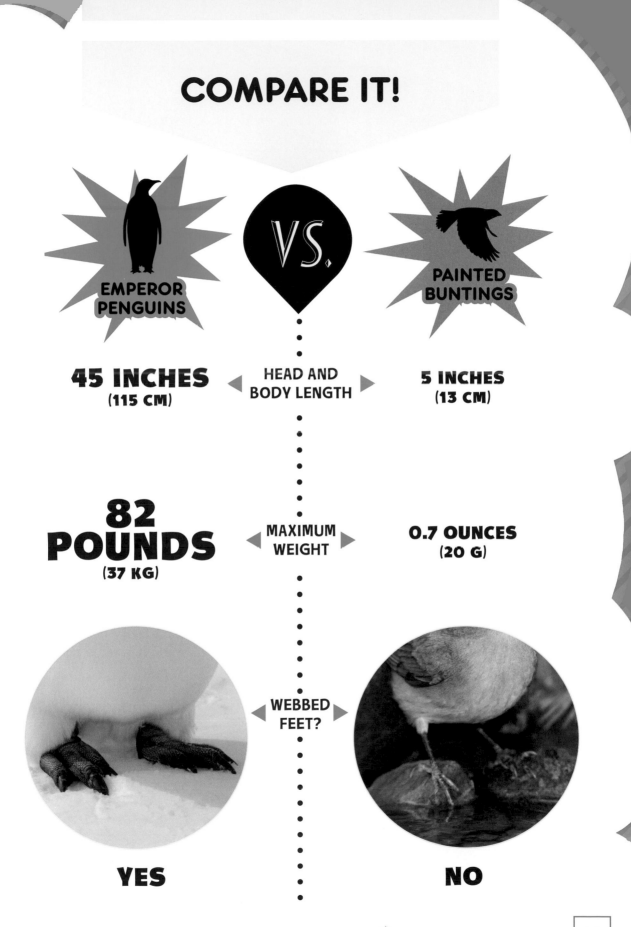

EMPEROR PENGUINS **VS.** PAINTED BUNTINGS

45 INCHES (115 CM) ◄ HEAD AND BODY LENGTH ► **5 INCHES** (13 CM)

82 POUNDS (37 KG) ◄ MAXIMUM WEIGHT ► **0.7 OUNCES** (20 G)

◄ WEBBED FEET? ►

YES **NO**

CHAPTER 2

WHERE DO EMPEROR PENGUINS LIVE?

Emperor penguins live in Antarctica near the South Pole. This continent is the coldest place on Earth. Emperor penguins are one of the few animals to live in this **habitat** year-round. They spend much of their lives near the coast, where it is warmer. Here, winter temperatures can drop down to about −22°F (−30°C). Further inland, it can be colder than −94°F (−70°C). Temperatures on the coast rise to an average of 32°F (0°C) in the summer.

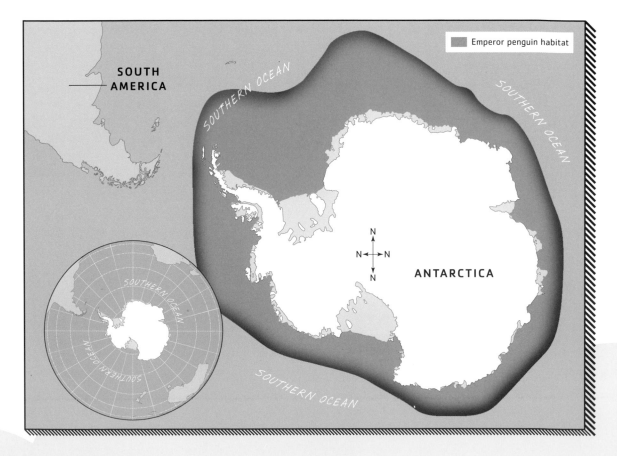

Emperor penguins are **adapted** to their polar habitat. Four layers of feathers cover most of their bodies. Icy wind and water can't get through. Emperor penguins also have a thick layer of fat under their skin. The feathers and fat keep these birds warm on land and at sea.

Emperor penguins are **carnivores**. They search the wintry Southern Ocean for fish, squid, and tiny creatures called **krill**. Emperor penguins can also be **prey**. They must watch out for hungry leopard seals and killer whales. These **predators** hunt in the waters around Antarctica.

EMPEROR PENGUINS VS. ANTARCTIC PETRELS

An Antarctic petrel soars just above the surface of the ocean. Suddenly it plunges its feet into the icy water to catch a fish. Antarctic petrels are brown and white hunting birds. Like Emperor penguins, they live on the coast of Antarctica. They also live on nearby islands and icebergs. That makes the petrel's habitat the same as the emperor penguin's.

Antarctic petrels hunt in Antarctica's ice-cold sea. Like emperor penguins, petrels are carnivores. They even eat the same kind of prey. Antarctic petrels hunt krill, fish, and squid.

An Antarctic petrel searches for something to eat.

COMPARE IT!

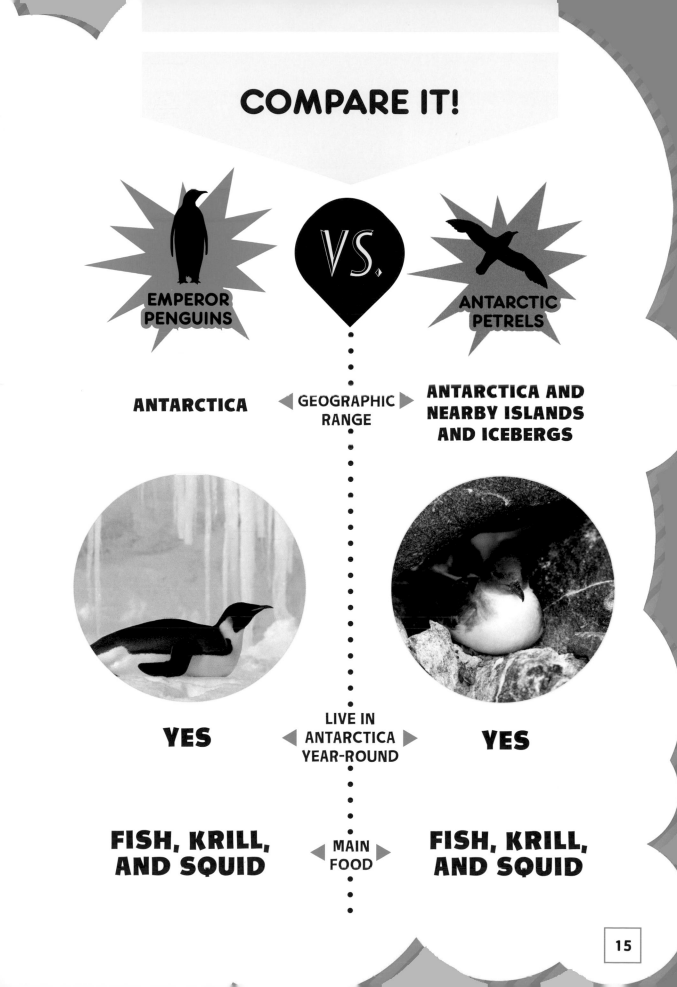

EMPEROR PENGUINS

VS.

ANTARCTIC PETRELS

ANTARCTICA	◄ GEOGRAPHIC RANGE ►	ANTARCTICA AND NEARBY ISLANDS AND ICEBERGS
YES	◄ LIVE IN ANTARCTICA YEAR-ROUND ►	**YES**
FISH, KRILL, AND SQUID	◄ MAIN FOOD ►	**FISH, KRILL, AND SQUID**

EMPEROR PENGUINS VS. SCARLET MACAWS

A scarlet macaw cracks open a nut with its powerful beak. Scarlet macaws live in tropical rain forests of North America and South America. This habitat differs greatly from that of emperor penguins.

The scarlet macaw's habitat stays warm all year long. There is also plenty of rain. More than 100 inches (254 cm) of rain can fall in rain forests each year. In comparison, Antarctica is a desert. It gets very little rain or snow.

DID YOU KNOW?
Scarlet macaws are
LEFT-FOOTED.
They use their left foot to grasp food as they eat.

Shrubs, trees, and other plants thrive in the scarlet macaw's moist environment. They provide food for this bird. Unlike penguins, the macaw is a herbivore. It eats fruits, nuts, seeds, and leaves. Tropical trees also provide protection for scarlet macaws. Perched up high, these birds are safe from predators roaming below.

CHAPTER 3
THE UNDERWATER HUNT OF EMPEROR PENGUINS

An emperor penguin swims deep underwater in search of prey. It spots a fish and zooms toward it. The penguin stretches out its thick neck. Then the bird snatches the fish in its long, pointy beak, feeding on the fish as it swims. The penguin is already searching for more prey.

Emperor penguins can dive deeper than any other diving bird. Emperor penguins can reach 1,850 feet (564 meters) below the

Emperor penguins dive for fish, squid, and krill.

DID YOU KNOW?
An emperor penguin's **MOUTH** works like a trap for prey. Its tongue and upper throat are covered with sharp spines. The spines keep squirmy prey from escaping.

surface of the water. They usually dive between 328 and 656 feet (100 and 200 m) to **forage** for food. They can also stay underwater longer than any other bird—more than twenty minutes.

Emperor penguins live in large groups called **colonies**. On land, they waddle on their webbed feet. They can also slide on their stomachs. Emperor penguins use their flippers to push their bodies along the slippery ice.

Emperor penguins slide on their bellies.

EMPEROR PENGUINS VS. BLACK SCOTERS

A black scoter zooms underwater to catch a crab. Black scoters are medium-size, dark-colored ducks. They spend most of their lives near coastlines. Both black scoters and emperor penguins are carnivores. They also hunt in similar ways.

Black scoters and emperor penguins are diving birds. They seek their prey under the water. Both birds have solid bones and are heavy enough to sink beneath the surface. And both use their webbed feet and wings to swim.

Like emperor penguins, black scoters are social birds. They hunt and live together in large groups. The birds help one another find good places to forage in the water. Living in a group also protects black scoters from predators.

Black scoters are strong swimmers.

COMPARE IT!

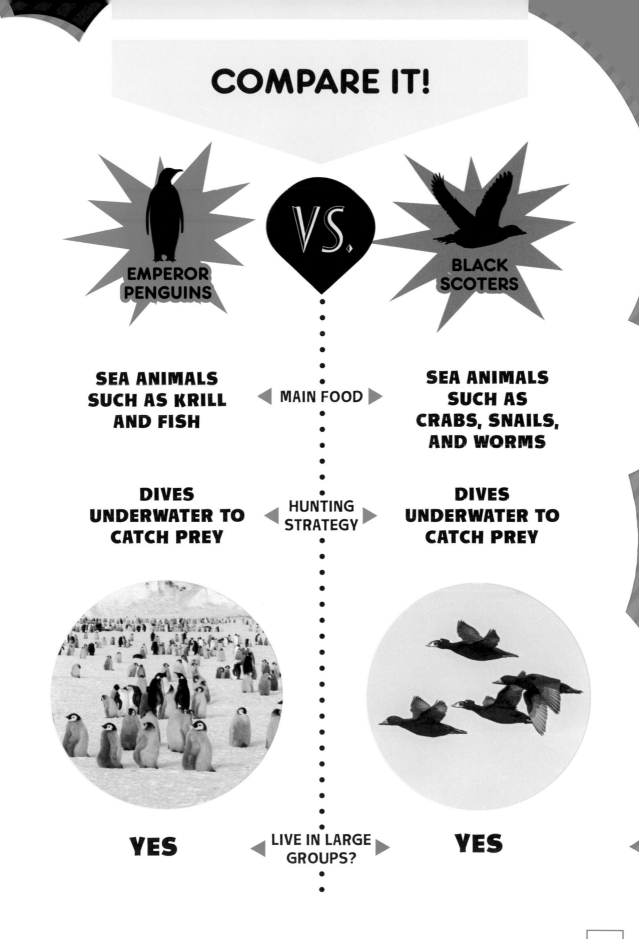

EMPEROR PENGUINS

VS.

BLACK SCOTERS

SEA ANIMALS SUCH AS KRILL AND FISH	◄ MAIN FOOD ►	SEA ANIMALS SUCH AS CRABS, SNAILS, AND WORMS
DIVES UNDERWATER TO CATCH PREY	◄ HUNTING STRATEGY ►	DIVES UNDERWATER TO CATCH PREY
YES	◄ LIVE IN LARGE GROUPS? ►	YES

EMPEROR PENGUINS VS. RED-TAILED HAWKS

A red-tailed hawk patiently watches a rabbit from a high branch. Suddenly the hawk takes flight and rockets toward the rabbit. Red-tailed hawks live in grasslands, forests, and deserts in North America. Their behavior differs from that of emperor penguins.

Red-tailed hawks have wide wingspans and sharp talons.

Red-tailed hawks don't dive for prey in the water the way emperor penguins do. The hawks use their powerful eyes to spy on squirrels, mice, and other small prey on land. When the time is right, the birds swoop down for a surprise attack. Red-tailed hawks catch prey in their sharp **talons**. The hawks tear the prey apart with their hooked beak and gulp down their meal quickly. Otherwise, another hungry bird might steal it.

Unlike emperor penguins, red-tailed hawks hunt alone. They don't live in large groups. One male and one female hawk often share a **territory**. They protect their young from predators. But adult hawks are fierce and have few predators.

CHAPTER 4

THE LIFE CYCLE OF EMPEROR PENGUINS

Emperor penguins return to their breeding grounds every year.
In March and April, they travel inland more than 50 miles (80 kilometers). There, the penguins pair up with a mate.

In May or June, a female penguin lays a single egg. Then she returns to sea. She will spend two months hunting for food to feed herself and her unborn chick. The male penguin stays behind. By this time, winter has begun in Antarctica. The male must incubate the egg and protect it from the cold. The egg rests on top of his feet, off the ice. He covers the egg with a warm pouch of his feathery skin. To keep his body warm, he huddles with other males in his colony.

DID YOU KNOW?
Male emperor penguins don't **EAT** while caring for their eggs. They lose up to half of their body weight during that time.

The egg hatches after
about two months.
By then, most of the
females have returned.
They feed their hungry chicks
by **regurgitating** food. The male
penguins are starving. They haven't
eaten for months. It's their turn to
go on a long feeding trip at sea.
Then they return to help raise their
chicks. Young emperor penguins set
out on their own after about 150
days. They are ready to mate
about five years later. Their
life span is about twenty
years in the wild.

EMPEROR PENGUINS VS. EMUS

An emu sprints across a grassland on long, powerful legs. Emus are large, flightless birds. They live in Australia. Emus and emperor penguins have similar life cycles.

As with emperor penguins, emus lay and incubate their eggs on land rather than in trees. A female emu lays up to twenty-four eggs in a shallow nest on the ground. She then leaves the nest behind. The male emu takes over. It's his job to incubate the eggs. Like male penguins, the emu eats nothing while he cares for his eggs. During this time, he may lose up to 33 percent of his body weight.

A male emu guards his eggs.

Emu chicks stay close to one another.

Emu eggs hatch after about fifty days. This is similar to the incubation period of emperor penguin eggs. The mother does not return after her chicks are born. The male emu raises them alone. Young emus set off on their own after about eighteen months. Emus live for an average of seven years in the wild.

DID YOU KNOW?
Emus can **RUN** faster than humans. The average emu can run up to 30 miles (48 km) per hour.

EMPEROR PENGUINS VS. RUBY-THROATED HUMMINGBIRD

A ruby-throated hummingbird flits about in search of **nectar** from flowers. Ruby-throated hummingbirds are tiny birds. They live in forests, prairies, and gardens in North America. They have a different life cycle than emperor penguins.

A male ruby-throated hummingbird **courts** a mate with a dramatic flying display. He loops and dives through the air above the female. A male emperor penguin can't fly. He attracts his mate with a special mating call.

After mating, the male ruby-throated hummingbird leaves and doesn't return. The female builds a nest in a tree. There she lays and incubates one to three tiny eggs. The eggs hatch after about two weeks. The chicks leave the nest for good about ten days later. Ruby-throated hummingbirds live for about nine years.

A ruby-throated hummingbird hovers near a flower.

COMPARE IT!

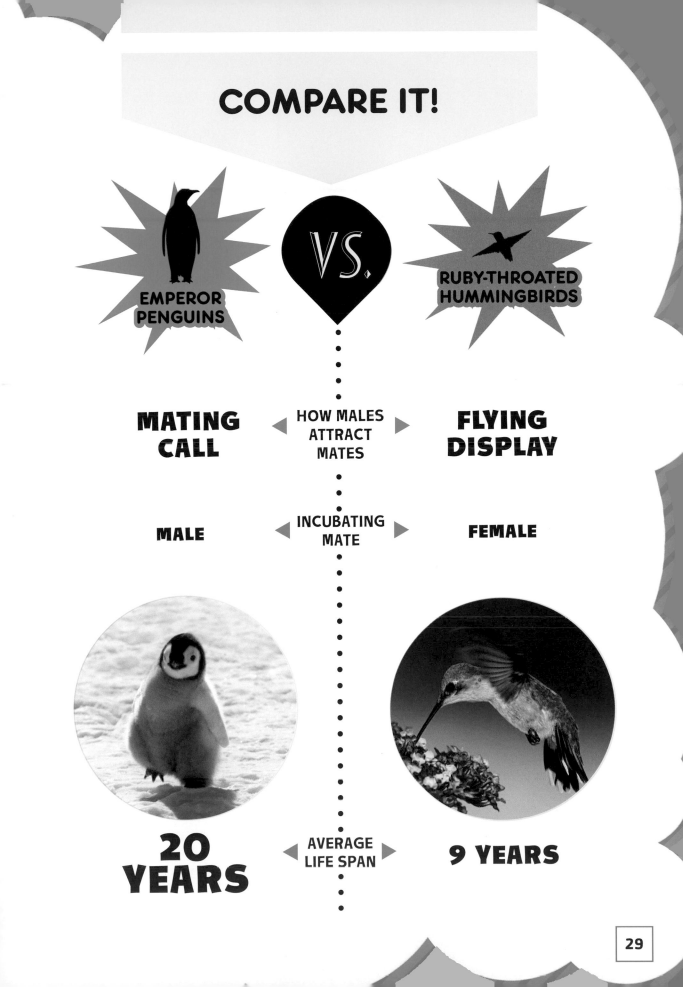

EMPEROR PENGUINS

VS.

RUBY-THROATED HUMMINGBIRDS

MATING CALL	◄ HOW MALES ATTRACT MATES ►	FLYING DISPLAY
MALE	◄ INCUBATING MATE ►	FEMALE
20 YEARS	◄ AVERAGE LIFE SPAN ►	9 YEARS

EMPEROR PENGUIN TRAIT CHART

This book introduces emperor penguins and compares them to other birds. What other birds would you like to compare?

	WARM-BLOODED	FEATHERS ON BODY	LAYS HARD-SHELLED EGGS	CARNIVORE	DIVES UNDERWATER	FLIGHTLESS BIRD
EMPEROR PENGUIN	X	X	X	X	X	X
ROYAL PENGUIN	X	X	X	X	X	X
PAINTED BUNTING	X	X	X			
ANTARCTIC PETREL	X	X	X	X	X	
SCARLET MACAW	X	X	X			
BLACK SCOTER	X	X	X	X	X	
RED-TAILED HAWK	X	X	X	X		
EMU	X	X	X			X
RUBY-THROATED HUMMINGBIRD	X	X	X			

GLOSSARY

adapted: suited to living in a particular environment

beak: the jaws and mouth of a bird. Beaks are sometimes called bills, especially when they are long and flat.

breeding grounds: places where animals go to produce offspring

camouflage: to hide or disguise an animal by covering it up or changing the way it looks

carnivores: meat-eating animals

colonies: groups of animals that live together and belong to one species

courts: behaves in a way meant to attract a mate

forage: to search for food

habitat: an environment where an animal naturally lives

herbivore: a plant-eating animal

incubate: to keep eggs warm and in good condition before they hatch

krill: small shrimplike animals that live in the ocean

nectar: sugary fluid found in plants

predators: animals that hunt, or prey on, other animals

prey: an animal that is hunted and killed by a predator for food

regurgitating: bringing swallowed food back up into the mouth

species: animals that share common features and can produce offspring

talons: the long, sharp claws of some hunting birds

territory: an area of land that is occupied and defended by an animal or a group of animals

traits: features that are inherited from parents. Body size and feather color are examples of inherited traits.

SELECTED BIBLIOGRAPHY

Dewey, Tanya. "*Aptenodytes forsteri*: Emperor Penguin." *Animal Diversity Web*. Last modified November 7, 2005. http://animaldiversity.org/accounts/Aptenodytes_forsteri.

"Emperor Penguins, *Aptenodytes forsteri*." MarineBio. Accessed March 12, 2015. http://marinebio.org/species.asp?id=534.

Lynch, Wayne. *Penguins of the World*. Buffalo: Firefly, 2007.

March of the Penguins. DVD. Directed by Luc Jacquet. Translated by Donnali Fifield. Washington, DC: National Geographic, 2006.

"Penguin." SeaWorld Parks & Entertainment. Accessed March 12, 2015. http://seaworld.org/en/animal-info/animal-infobooks/penguin.

FURTHER INFORMATION

Johnson, Jinny. *Animal Planet™ Atlas of Animals*. Minneapolis: Millbrook Press, 2012. Travel around the world and explore the planet's incredible animal diversity in this richly illustrated book.

National Geographic: Fishing with Emperor Penguins http://video.nationalgeographic.com/video/crittercam/wc-fishing-emperor-penguins Watch this video to see how emperor penguins dive and hunt for fish underwater.

Walker, Sally M. *Frozen Secrets: Antarctica Revealed*. Minneapolis: Carolrhoda Books, 2010. Learn what scientists and explorers have discovered about the harsh habitat that emperor penguins and other animals call home.

Wildscreen Arkive: Emperor Penguin (*Aptenodytes forsteri*) http://www.arkive.org/emperor-penguin/aptenodytes-forsteri Learn more about the lives of emperor penguins with this website's photos, videos, and facts.

INDEX